# YOU
## Were M...

David Wilbourne ... in
Yorkshire and studie... before
returning to the dio... ish priest.
During a 20-year minis... hospital chaplain, worked in parishes ... esbrough and near
Pontefract and for six years... ved as chaplain to two
Archbishops of York, John Habgood and David Hope,
before moving in 1997 to his present post as vicar of
the moors market town of Helmsley. David is a much
sought after spiritual director, visiting preacher, confer-
ence speaker, retreat leader and radio broadcaster,
and includes in his research interests New Testament
textual criticism and the trial of Christ.

As well as being a regular *Church Times* diarist, his
previous publications include *Archbishop's Diary*
(SPCK, 1995), *A Virgin's Diary* (Azure, 1999), *A
Vicar's Diary* (HarperCollins, 1998) and its sequel *A
Summer's Diary* (HarperCollins, 2001).

He is married to Rachel, a history and RE teacher,
and they have three daughters. His hobbies include
cycling (despite the steep moors), tennis, table tennis,
campanology and hill walking.

*For Geoff Jenkinson,*
*Headteacher of Ryedale School,*
*our local comprehensive school,*
*and his team, in gratitude*
*for all your hard work in encouraging*
*pupils to flourish and blossom.*

# YOU
# Were Made For
# ME

David Wilbourne

**TRIANGLE**

Published in Great Britain in 2001 by
Triangle
Society for Promoting Christian Knowledge
Holy Trinity Church
Marylebone Road
London NW1 4DU

Scripture quotations taken from the Holy Bible,
New International Version copyright © 1973, 1978, 1984
by International Bible Society. Used by permission of
Hodder & Stoughton Ltd.

*British Library Cataloguing-in-Publication Data*

A catalogue record for this book is available from
the British Library

ISBN 0-281-05427-4

Typeset by Pioneer Associates, Perthshire
Printed in Great Britain by
Omnia Books, Glasgow

# Contents

# Introduction

Though I have always been conscious that I do not pray enough, the more I pray, the more I am aware of two things. The first is that God is exceedingly complex, which is what you'd expect, really, God being God. As Somerset Maugham said, 'A god who can be understood is no god.' The second discovery that dawns on me as I pray is that I am exceedingly complex, too, and that somehow the key to my complexity lies in him.

This Lent book explores the complicated strands of our personality, an exploration which began as a series of lunchtime Lent lectures at York Minster, attended by a wide cross-section of people, from theology professors to office workers popping in during their lunch hour, from nuns to agnostics. So, the content had to be like a stream in which a mouse could paddle and an elephant could swim. Since then I have rewritten the lectures and expanded them considerably, but tried to retain their original characteristic – exploring deep issues of faith with a light touch.

We use names for others and ourselves that slip

off our lips unthinkingly: I, it, you, we, they, me. We call them personal pronouns, a title that often hides the impersonal way in which they are used. What do these names mean, though, and what can they mean when linked to the path Christ walked from his temptations to Golgotha and beyond? This book meditates on all the personal pronouns, combining homely stories with theology, as it takes us through Lent to Holy Week and onwards.

This book is dedicated to the Headteacher and staff of Ryedale School, our local comprehensive here in the shadow of the North York Moors. During my four years' connection with the school, I have been particularly struck by the major way all the teachers there enable human flourishing in their disparate charges, so, given the book's theme of developing personality, the dedication seems particularly appropriate.

Imagine the scene: a bunfight in some ecclesiastical backwater, the dingy church hall packed with folk, the purple-cassocked Archbishop of York circulating animatedly among them. I am standing on the edge of the crowd, pretending that I'm playing a John the Baptist to my boss's Jesus, decreasing so he can increase. Actually, I'm a shy person standing beside another shy person, both of us desperately trying to think of something to say. 'Are you the Vicar, then?' my companion on the edge of the crowd eventually stutters.

'No, I'm the Archbishop's chaplain,' I reply.

'An archbishop's chaplain? What's an archbishop's chaplain?' he asks, seizing on this topic of conversation like a drowning man being thrown a rope. Unfortunately his eagerness means that he doesn't quite get the right tone of voice. I detect a hint of accusation there, as if he were an assiduous customs' official and I was an asylum seeker flaunting a bogus career on my passport.

'I'm a cross between a Bernard and a Sir Humphrey, of *Yes, Prime Minister* fame,' I quip, trying to be jolly. My attempt falls flat as my companion has never seen *Yes, Prime Minister*, so hasn't got a clue what I'm going on about. An awkward silence surges softly backwards, punctuated by the munching of bought-in quiche, tepid and well past its sell-by date.

To be fair to him, my job was rare enough to floor even the most experienced *What's My Line?* panel, with the whole of the Church of England only boasting two archbishop's chaplains. While I was far more of a Bernard than a Sir Humphrey, quite a lot of my job entailed getting into the mindset of the archbishop so I could run with his vision and keep the shop going during his many absences.

Mind you, getting into an archbishop's mindset is quite an addiction, and I have found myself being intrigued not just by the two archbishops I worked for, but by any archbishop, voraciously consuming archiepiscopal biographies so I could try to fathom their essence, seeking clues as to what made them tick. Was Archbishop William Fitzherbert really dispatched by a duplistic archdeacon slipping a poisonous draught into his communion wine? What precisely did Archbishop Lancelot Blackburn get up to in his previous career as a pirate? Was Archbishop Edwin Sandys really totally innocent when another man's wife was found in his bed?

Was Archbishop Vernon Harcourt really wise to lower the ceiling of his palace chapel to form bedrooms for his 16 children or did he like his prayers invaded by the patter of 32 tiny feet? We can only conjecture.

Modern archbishops are no less intriguing. What was in Archbishop Cyril Garbett's mind as he was carried ashore by six muscular natives, sedan chair-style, in Papua New Guinea, with thousands on the beach kneeling for his blessing? Equally, what was in Michael Ramsey's labyrinth of a mind as he wandered off from an ecclesiastical procession, changed his trousers and then rejoined it? What was in Archbishop John Habgood's eight-year-old mind as he penned a letter to God, inviting him to stay in the spare room and bathe with the family?

Of course, it's not just archbishops' chaplains who want to delve into their masters' mindsets and catch their essence. Humphrey Carpenter's scandalous biography of the late Robert Runcie was made even more delicious because it contained transcripts of indiscreet statements by the former archbishop, recorded on a tape recorder. Surely, the argument went, this caught the *real* Runcie, verbatim stuff. No need for a biographer's conjecture here. The tape recorder could hardly lie; after all, it provides evidence so objective that the prosecution could use it in a court of law.

Transcripts of recordings might seem the key to unlocking the essence of anyone, whether arch-bishop or not. Taking that argument to its ultimate conclusion, if somehow the machinations and con-versations going on in my head could be recorded, then that record would chart the essential me, would provide irrefutable evidence of what I am, when the veneers and the selves I would so like to project are totally stripped away.

Of course, with the sorry tale of Joan of Arc before us, we are all wary of admitting to hearing voices or allowing that we take too much notice of them. Yet, if we are honest, we know that conver-sations not only go on in our minds, but also are the quintessence of any thought process. Points are put, counter-points are made and we deliberate and muddle through to a conclusion. Sometimes the debate is so adversarial that it is like Question Time in Parliament is going on inside our heads, com-plete with 'Hear, hears' and 'Boos' and 'Gentlemen, order please!' as our own 'government' and 'opposi-tion' vie for supremacy.

Where the voices come from is devastatingly difficult to discern. Some are a straight replay from childhood. What my parents, what my teachers said to me in childhood I find myself repeating to my own children in times of panic or frustration or when I think I'm being wise:

4

'You'll catch pneumonia if you don't put your shoes and socks on!'

'You are not to leave that nice boiled fish; we cannot afford to waste it!'

Times have moved on, though. Bare feet will not instantly court pneumonia in a centrally heated house, even if it is the last old and damp and decrepit vicarage in captivity. Clerical incomes may not be luxurious, but financial ruin does not now hinge on a few scraps of uneaten fish. Yet the voices remain, out of context, passed on from generation to generation.

They have other sources, too. There's a galaxy of incidents that you imagine have been long forgotten, until your memory is suddenly triggered by a sight, a sound, a touch, a smell. A glimpse of a mountain will replay a conversation buried for 20 years, even down to the nuance in each word. The fragrance of a crushed ear of wheat will fast-rewind you to childhood, with the clamour of your playmates thronging your cerebral airwaves. Yet another syrupy TV programme on pop nostalgia will catapult you back decades, so that once again you're an adolescent jiving on the dance floor with sweet nothings being whispered in your now middle-aged ear.

Then there are snippets from reading, listening, watching, with scripture, hymns, prayers, stored

5

deep down, all consciously or unconsciously absorbed by your multimedia centre par excellence, welling up when the right recall key is pressed. Not to mention that lurking within you, the moods and the anger and the storms that would have turned into a lion or a tiger had the evolutionary process gone another way.

All form a waveband of voices that my mind is constantly scanning. Put the voices on tape and you've got what I am, the definitive David Wilbourne – or have you? Surely it's not so much my voices, but, rather, what I do with them that makes me what I am. Descartes claimed that *cogito, ergo sum* – I think, therefore I am – was the essence of existence. Maybe 'I select, therefore I am' is a more refined definition.

I guess that 28 centuries ago in the year King Uzziah died, the prophet Isaiah was faced with such a choice and was defined by the path he selected. I like to picture him going into the temple with myriad voices ringing in his ears, 'What are you doing here?' Uzziah had reigned for a comparatively stable and prosperous 52 years. In a very long, rather depressing and mostly unpronounceable list, Uzziah was one of the few kings of Israel who 'did what was right in the eyes of the Lord'. Then, suddenly, King Uzziah was dead, society was breaking down, the 12 tribes of Israel were at loggerheads, yet again, with the barbarians at the gates, ready to gobble them up. A scene disturbingly familiar to us, bombarded as we are with change and instability, inside and outside the Middle East.

So Isaiah enters the temple. 'What am I doing here when all this religion stuff is so irrelevant? Why aren't I outside, doing something useful, seeking allies, sharpening the spear, tensing the bow?'

Then another voice, 'What am I doing here when I am so unworthy to make even a faltering step towards God's presence? I am a man of unclean lips, I live among a people of unclean lips . . .'

Such adversarial voices tear through him, but do not constrain him. Isaiah is actually defined by harnessing the voices and selecting his magnificent assent that has rung down the millennia: 'Here am I. Send me!' (Isaiah 6.8)

As with Isaiah, so, supremely, we see this with Jesus, too, as there were adversarial voices in his mind. This becomes particularly significant when you remember that 'adversary' in Hebrew is *Satana*:

The tempter came to him and said, 'If you are the Son of God, tell these stones to become bread.' (Matthew 4.3)

The turning of stones into bread voiced a subtle invitation to use his mission and his miraculous power to take his own cut, to feather his own nest, to make sure he was taken care of, and taken care of well. 'Go on, you owe it to yourself . . .'

> Again, the devil took him to a very high mountain and showed him all the kingdoms of the world and their splendour. 'All this I will give you', he said, 'if you will bow down and worship me.' (Matthew 4.8–9)

A subversive whisper for Jesus to give up on all this airy-fairy religious stuff and, instead, sell out to secular powers and their values. Why be an itinerant carpenter in a third-rate state when you could be a multinational hero?

> Then the devil took him to the holy city and had him stand on the highest point of the temple. 'If you are the Son of God,' he said, 'throw yourself down . . .' (Matthew 4.5–6)

Leaping off the temple is a siren song, tempting Jesus to gain popularity by pulling stunts (after all, even Paul Daniels has his fans). It can be linked with other siren songs, such as Jesus' words in the Garden of Gethsemane on Maundy Thursday: 'My Father, if it is possible, may this cup be taken from me' (Matthew 26.39) and even his words from the cross: 'My God, my God, why have you forsaken me?' (Matthew 27.46)

In a sense, these voices are those of bad theology, encouraging an idea of an Entebbe-raid God who snatches people off crosses rather than a God who stays on the cross, impaled on the pain. God is not at the top of the tower goading you on to do silly things; rather, he lies mangled at the bottom of the tower, wondering how you could have been so stupid in the first place.

Those invitations, then, did not make Jesus what he was. What made him was his response to them. In the wilderness he said:

> . . . Man does not live on bread alone, but on every word that comes from the mouth of God. (Matthew 4.4)

> . . . Worship the Lord your God, and serve him only . . . (Matthew 4.10)

> . . . Do not put the Lord your God to the test. (Matthew 4.7)

> . . . Away from me, Satan! . . . (Matthew 4.10)

In the Garden of Gethsemane he said:

> . . . Yet not as I will, but as you will. (Matthew 26.39)

On the cross, he selected Psalm 31 for his magisterial, 'Father, into your hands I commit my spirit' (Luke 23.46).

Resolutely setting himself Godwards, he was able to harness the voices to focus on his vocation. By 'vocation' I mean having the nerve to be the 'I' that God intended.

I choose my words carefully. Harness the voices rather than banish them or pretend they were never there. Jesus heard adversarial voices from outside as well as from inside:

What is the greatest commandment?

But who is my neighbour?

One woman for seven brothers; whose wife will she be in heaven?

Is it lawful to pay taxes to Caesar or not?

In his play *Son of Man*, Dennis Potter has Jesus replying to the last question as follows:

Then give to Caesar what belongs to Caesar. And give to God what belongs to God. And shut up!

Funny though the surprise ending is, and tempted though we may be to use exactly the same words against those adversaries whose ravings weary us so much, I sense Potter misses the spirit of Christ here, which was actually fashioned by responding to the voices. No voices, no fashioning. No fashioning, no formation. No formation, no 'I' as we know him to be. The essence of Christ, that which opens

10

us to the possibility of salvation for all, is that he engaged with the voices; he did not banish them.

Nor did he pretend they never were. One of Christianity's immensely redeeming features is that its founder, in three out of the four Gospels, begins his ministry by hearing voices, conferring a God-given dignity on the phenomenon. An undoubted state of maturity is to realize that what I am is not set in concrete, but is subject to change, development, ebbs and flows. Yet, we have this peculiar obsession with constancy. 'The lady's not for turning!' was seen as Margaret Thatcher's greatest accolade, whereas 'unstable', 'unpredictable', 'changeable' are usually used in a derogatory sense. However, haven't we got it the wrong way round? Shouldn't the most massive words in a political scene, or in any scene come to that, be, 'I was so wrong. Forgive me. I've changed my mind and it's going to stay changed'?

John's Gospel, of course, does not start with Jesus hearing any voices, yet the pattern of Jesus' ministry in John suggests that the voices are there and, in many ways, parallel the temptations in the wilderness. He starts as a protégé of John the Baptist, a firebrand, an Ian Paisley of Palestine, overturning tables, deriding the commercialism of religion, denouncing Israel's wicked ways, warning of the coming Kingdom. Then comes a sea change

11

so drastic that even John fails to recognize his former pupil. Now a man of the people, who pities the crowd, who champions the underdog, Jesus seems set to become their non-violent king, in a kingdom where 'liberation', not 'catastrophe', is the key word. However, another sea change comes when Jesus resists coronation by popular assent and, instead, takes a donkey and sits on it, setting himself on a path of humility that can only lead to the cross.

It seems that the only one in history to call himself 'I am' only became 'I am' by working through possibilities, both hypothetical and actual. The key trait is the openness to God – the early mornings, the quiet places, the long hours of prayer, the sensitivity to situations that surprised him on his path, the Gethsemanes and Golgothas where the voices and choices are put in perspective when set against the one in whom we move and have our being.

Though I am more than my voices and choices, I do not despise them as I believe that, through them, God and his silence can fashion the 'I' he wants me to be. Of course, the crunch issue is how to decide whether the call we hear is from God or something more sinister. A useful three-fold check is to be gleaned from Paul in 1 Corinthians, who was addressing a group verging on charismatic anarchy, with the Spirit allegedly authorizing them to do all sorts of strange things.

1. Is what God's Spirit is inspiring you to do consonant with the personality of Christ? Despite the Gospels being ravaged by critical scholarship, they still present a strong character profile of Christ that enables us intuitively to say, when faced with other pictures of him, from something like the Apocryphal Gospels, 'Yes, this is him to a tee' or 'No, this misses him by a mile.' Does what you hear God saying square with the man who welcomed the outcast, who touched and healed the untouchables, who told stories of lost sheep and lost sons and lost coins, of good fathers and good shepherds and good Samaritans, who died forgiving his tormentors, breathing to the convicted terrorist dying beside him, 'Today you will be with me in paradise', exuding forgiveness to the very last? Does the ultimate voice you select jar with that man or ride easily with him? Paul pulls no punches when he concludes that if the Spirit who rules your every day inspires you to say 'Christ be cursed', then it just isn't God's spirit.

2. Is what God's Spirit inspires going to build up God's people? Sometimes it is necessary to knock down in order to build up, to prune in

13

order to promote growth, but is what you are inspired to do ultimately going to promote a better structure or are you actually into destroying things because you're dominated by a destructive streak? How can you let that destructive streak go and find another voice?

3. Is what God's Spirit inspires consonant with the pattern of sacrificial love outlined in 1 Corinthians 13? A love that keeps no score of wrongs, a love that does not gloat over other people's sins, is patient, kind and never boastful . . . How does that square with the voice you have selected?

Of course, Paul's three criteria do not provide an exhaustive check, nor are they above criticism, but they have been validated over two millennia as giving us a very good start to sifting through the influences that drive us each and every day. At the end of each of those days of so many voices, the essential archbishop and the essential Runcie and the essential each one of us is not to be found in the gabbling, but in the divine pauses by which the talk and action are judged and purified.

Almighty God,
to whom all hearts are open,
all desires known,
and from whom no secrets are hidden:

cleanse the thoughts of our hearts
by the inspiration of your Holy Spirit,
that we may perfectly love you,
and worthily magnify your holy name;
through Christ our Lord. Amen.

Prayer of Preparation in Order One,<br>
*Common Worship*

## For further reflection

- Are there any other biblical figures who engage with adversarial voices to sharpen their vocation?
- Can you think of a situation in the recent life of the Church where debate that seemed wearisome and polarized has actually been harnessed to move things forward?
- What Gethsemanes and Golgothas are there in your own experience – tragedies where the voices and choices have ultimately given way to God's will?
- Are there any situations you have been in when you have wondered whether the voice you have heard is God's or not? What checks have you used?

# 2 | It

St Martin le Grand in Coney Street in York had been severely damaged in the vicious Baedecker raids in the last war. In a sermon celebrating its restoration, Archbishop John Habgood had quoted from a striking poem by Alan Paton, of *Cry, the Beloved Country* fame, called 'Meditation for a Young Boy Confirmed'. During the short drive back to Bishopthorpe Palace afterwards, I braved breaking the usual heavy silence and asked him where the poem could be found. '*Theology*, August 1958,' he replied, in the sort of frosty voice an experienced vet would reserve for a new boy who had asked, 'Where precisely is a dog's backbone?' The undoubted implication was that I really shouldn't trouble him with such basics.

While I was only two years old in August 1958 and hadn't quite developed sufficiently to take *Theology*, my wife's late mother had taken the journal and had bequeathed to us her back copies, so I was able to quickly trace the poem, which I have been hooked on ever since. It is an undoubted epic of *Ancient Mariner* proportions, its 16 stanzas covering six of the journal's 40 pages, and touching in depth on almost every aspect of faith and life, of loving and losing, of worship and wasting. Take, for instance, stanza 9:

Do not pronounce judgement on the Infinite;
nor suppose God to be like a bad Prime Minister,
Do not suppose him powerless,
or if powerful malignant.
Do not address your mind to criticism
    of the Creator,
do not pretend to know his categories.
Do not take his Universe in your hand,
and point out its defects with condescension.
Do not think he is a greater potentate,
a manner of President of the United Galaxies.
Do not think that because you know so few
    human beings,
that he is in a comparable though more
    favourable position.
Do not think it absurd that he should know
    every sparrow,
or the number of the hairs of your head.
Do not compare him with yourself,
nor suppose your human love to be an
    example to shame him.
He is not greater than Plato or Lincoln,
nor superior to Shakespeare and Beethoven;

He is their God, their powers and their
  gifts proceeded from him,
In infinite darkness they pored with their
  fingers
over the first word of the Book of Knowledge.

Alan Paton, 'Meditation for a Young Boy Confirmed'

I suppose Alan Paton is warning his son against treating God as an 'it'. By that I mean regarding God as a convenient object on to whom we can project our self-interest, our prejudices, our desires, our limited thought processes: philosophies and theologies constrained by our mortal horizons.

Alan Paton's stanza reminds me of another poem, 'In Westminster Abbey', by Sir John Betjeman, where a well-heeled woman steals into the dark abbey during wartime and visits all her prejudices on God, taking his universe in her hand and readily pointing out its defects with condescension. She has the audacity to conclude with, 'What a treat to hear thy word where the bones of leading statesmen have so often been interr'd', when poor God hadn't been able to get a word in edgeways because of her incessant chatter. She treats God as a convenient object, an 'it' rather than a 'you' to be reckoned with and encountered.

Her mis-prayer judges us all because, to a greater or lesser extent, we all play that game. I think of public intercession in a church service where God is talked down to and informed of the state of play in the world, as if he were a backward child who has to have the news spelt out for him. 'O God, you are not a *Times* or a *Telegraph* reader, I fear, so let me tell you all about it. Now, are you listening carefully?'

Once our parish Lent group trawled through Gerard Hughes' *God of Surprises* and came up with some surprises itself. One exercise invited us to take God's universe in hand and point out its defects. Taking my cue from Job 42, I expected an awesome and penitential silence. Instead, the floodgates were opened and complaints flowed with the heady glee of a Ken Livingstone given free rein to criticize Tony Blair. Concerns were age-old and focused on the sheer unfairness of a creation stacked in favour of some rather than others. Tongue in cheek, I invited the group to think of creation as a company, The Universe plc, with its managing director summoned to defend all its shortcomings on BBC's *Watchdog*. 'But Anne Robinson would crucify him!' someone exclaimed, unintentionally summarizing most of the doctrine of the atonement and our misperceptions of it in one priceless quip.

To take another illustration, from time to time I receive odd phone calls. Recently a woman aired her concern to me about psychic vicars who might manipulate fellow psychics, like her and her children, in their congregation. 'People don't go to church to be manipulated or disturbed; they go for a bit of comfort,' she commented, as if she were stating the obvious.

After listening patiently to her for 25 minutes, I could restrain myself no longer. 'Never mind psychic vicars,' I pointed out. 'You risk far worse than that by going to church. The almighty, all-terrible God could unleash himself on you, could change you irrevocably, for ever, could demand from you the highest sacrifice, that you take up your cross and follow him.' She terminated the call pretty quickly after that, convinced that her neurosis paled into insignificance when compared to mine.

Yet we have to let God be God, let him make us in his image rather than we make him in ours, let him judge and fashion us rather than we judge and fashion him. Let God be God; never devalue him by letting him be 'it'. Much has been written about Jesus boldly addressing God as 'Abba', an Aramaic form of address that approximates to our 'Daddy' and brings with it a healthy and life-giving intimacy between creature and creator. Yet the downside of this is that we can treat God as the sort of daddy whom we can twist around our little finger, the beleaguered daddy who is hostage to the every whim of his spoilt child, like the hapless father of the aptly named Verruca in *Charlie and the Chocolate*

*Factory* who has no existence other than being a slave to her childish and selfish desires. We need to be reminded that the first petition of our Lord's Prayer goes 'Our Father, who art *in heaven*'. In other words, the intimate relationship we are privileged to have access to has to be necessarily balanced by the breath-taking realization of just who this is we are relating to – almighty God, heaven's king, no less.

Letting God be the God of heaven also includes letting his will be done on earth, avoiding treating his creation as merely an object. The environment that God made and God makes is not there for us to exploit and use for our own petty purposes. If we pause to regard it rather than trample it down, it can actually beckon to us, deepening our knowledge of who we are and how much we receive. 'The flashing of the lightning free, the whirling wind's tempestuous shocks', in the ancient poem 'St Patrick's Breastplate', could be harnessed for our purposes, could power our machines. However, that is not why they feature. Rather, they form part of a Celtic Benedicite where all God's works are literally worthy of praise and are therefore to be treated accordingly. 'The stable earth, the deep salt sea, around the old eternal rocks' deserve reverence, not to be written off as 'it'.

As with things, so with people:

'It is extraordinary how we betray our friends. Or (as we think in our conceited minds) it is not extraordinary at all. For we, of course, are superior persons, viewing mankind from a great height, and awarding our acquaintances praise and blame with poetic justice, if not with justice, anyhow with such charm, that even malice ought to be forgiven us.'

Austin Farrer catches well an all too prevalent tendency to set ourselves as judge over the rest of the human race, to treat other people as objects, actors and actresses in a play, the script of which only we can write. Yet the heart of the Christian gospel is that we are all God's children and therefore all deserve the respect due to children of God. When we demean other people and use them as a means to an end, be that end our financial well-being or our self-promotion or our personal or sexual gratification, when we fail to encounter them as fellow children of God, then it is our own existence as well as theirs that we pervert. If we deny other people the privilege of being a subject and always treat them as objects, then our own claim to subject status is nullified by our own actions.

It may seem strange to say – as I make a plea for upholding the sacredness of God and the sacredness of creation and the sacredness of those we encounter – that I believe that Jesus actually came to abolish the sacred. However, such a shocking statement has a proviso: he came to abolish the sacred by making everything sacred.

Think about how he started, by being born in a cowshed where his birth was hailed by shepherds. We may have a rosy, rustic view of shepherds, but, in the strict Pharisaic scheme of things, they were outcasts. They not only watched their flocks by night, but also on the sabbath, breaking the fourth commandment. They wandered into unclean Gentile territory, defiling themselves to seek their lost sheep. Flashback to King David's anointing in 1 Samuel 16, when seven of Jesse's sons are paraded before Samuel for him to choose Israel's monarch. David's profession as a shepherd was so contemptible that his father didn't even mention him until heavily prompted by the prophet:

> ... Are these all the sons you have? (1 Samuel 16.11)

Drawing a response that is sneeringly dismissive:

> There is still the youngest ... but he is tending the sheep. ... (1 Samuel 16.11)

Samuel, though, persists:

> ... Send for him; we will not sit down until he arrives. (1 Samuel 16.11)

So he is sent for and brought in. He was ruddy with

a fine appearance and handsome features. '. . . Then the Lord said, "Rise and anoint him; he is the one." So Samuel took the horn of oil and anointed him in the presence of his brothers, and from that day on the Spirit of the Lord came upon David in power. . . .' (1 Samuel 16.12–13).

Note that in 1 Samuel 16, the name 'David' isn't even mentioned until the end of the narrative. In the oral tradition in which this story originally circulated, this would have made for high drama, begging the question, 'Who can this nobody, this forgotten child, be?' Then all is revealed in the final reel, 'Goodness, this is no less than David, our beloved David, Israel's greatest king.' It is also significant that it is only after God's anointing that David is named, is given his worth. Written off even by his family as an 'it', a nothing, just a boy who did the dirty work, God turns the tables and turns object into subject.

Just as the tables were overturned by Jesus' birth, those who were outcasts according to human schemes suddenly found themselves not cast out according to God's scheme, but, rather, cast in, in mighty roles. Conferring a sacredness on what hitherto had been deemed outside God's scope was a major part of the drama of Jesus' birth and was to become his trademark: something written off as an 'it' is transformed into something immense, to be encountered.

This theme permeated Jesus' mission as a man. By mixing with the riff-raff, quislings, tax collectors, prostitutes, sinners, by being anointed by a woman of the streets, he hammered home the message that those allegedly outside God's law were not outside by his standards, but had an honoured place in his eyes.

He really hammered home that message by allowing the nails to be hammered through his own flesh on the cross. By being executed as a common criminal, even his death carries his trademark idea as he turns a curse into a blessing. He conferred a sacredness on what hitherto had been seen as the last place where sacredness could be found. 'Cursed is he who hangs on a tree,' the Torah had proclaimed, but this was not proclaimed by our Lord as he stayed on the cross. His crucifixion advertises that the world's squalor and pain is not outside God's matrix, but, rather, that God is actually impaled on it, immersed in it. Calvary shouts that God is not some divine touch-judge, watching the match from an aloof and safe distance, a harsh disciplinarian ready to intervene when the rules are breached. Rather, he is actually involved, and involved intimately, in the field of play. By looming large in those very situations that, hitherto, God was thought to shun, Jesus, through his litany of commonality, conferred a sanctity, a dignity on them all. To quote stanza 11 of Alan Paton's poem:

Such was the brief, such was the lonely life,
Such was the bondage of the earth, such was
   the misery,
Such was the reaching out, such was the
   separation,
That my Lord tore the curtain from the skies,
   and in compassion
He took upon himself all angry things,
the scourge, the thorn, the nail, the utter
   separation;
and spoke such words as made me tremble,
and laid his yoke upon me,
and bound me with these chains,
that I have worn with no especial grace.

   Alan Paton, 'Meditation for a Young Boy Confirmed'

I suppose the most moving example of all this is
Mary's experience by the tomb on Easter morning:

At this, she turned round and saw Jesus standing
there, but she did not realize that it was Jesus.
'Woman,' he said, 'why are you crying? Who is
it you are looking for?' Thinking he was the
gardener, she said, 'Sir, if you have carried him
away, tell me where you have put him, and I
will get him.' Jesus said to her, 'Mary.' She
turned towards him and cried out in Aramaic,
'Rabboni!' (which means Teacher). (John
20.14–16)

Speculation has been rife about Mary Magdalene for the 2000 years of the history of Christianity. From the Gospels right down to *Jesus Christ Superstar*, she has been a mysterious figure with a certain past in the shadows. Was she the anonymous woman of ill repute who washed Jesus' feet at the house of Simon the Pharisee, the woman who had been forgiven much so had much to give? Was she another anonymous woman who stole into the inner circle of the disciples and anointed Jesus' head with expensive oil, incurring the disciples' wrath for such extravagance? Was she the Mary of Mary, Martha and Lazarus fame, who sat devotedly listening to Jesus while her sister did the housework single-handed? Certainly Luke tells us that Jesus cast seven devils out of her. Whether this is a pious euphemism for the fact that she was a prostitute or that she was deranged in some other way, we simply don't know. Even so, seven devils represents the highest score on the possession stakes.

Whatever her previous life, she would have been treated as an object, an object to avoid, an object to shun, an object to abuse. She would have been called many names: slag, tart, nutter, weirdo, scum, piece of dirt. I suspect that hardly ever would she have been addressed as Mary. The risen Jesus, in invoking her real name, in calling her Mary, cuts through all that prejudice at a stroke. An object no longer, she is a distinct person in the eyes of the one whose eyes are the only ones that count. Little wonder that John describes her turning twice: not just a physical turning, but also a turning of heart and mind as she rejoices at her true value.

It is striking that in one of the Genesis accounts of creation, in Paradise before the Fall, Adam names all the creatures of the world as they are brought before him. Their distinctness is recognized as each is given a name, a worth to be encountered and valued rather than exploited. Jesus, given the title the new Adam by Paul, paves the way for Paradise's restoration as he calls Mary by name. As he bestows on Mary her worth, he can also do it for all of us, only hoping that we catch the habit and do it for others, banishing 'it' for ever.

It was probably fitting that I first encountered Alan Paton's magisterial poem at a service celebrating St Martin le Grand's restoration. The building had been a bomber's target, was treated as an 'it', a thing to be laid waste as spoil of a vicious war, standing as a ruin for decades until it was rebuilt and transformed into a place to be revered.

I suppose its recent history stands as an icon for us all, a journey from convenient object to treasured subject. It is a necessary journey, so that our perception of God, our perception of people and things around us and, ultimately, our perception of ourselves may blossom and make for the flourishing that God desires.

## For further reflection

- David, shepherds, Mary Magdalene: are there any other biblical figures who follow the path from being written off as an 'it' to being encountered as sacred?
- Can you think of a situation in which individuals or causes are written off as an 'it' rather than encountered as sacred:
  – within secular life
  – within the Church
  – in your own personal experience?
  What are you going to do to change things?
- 'Christ abolished the sacred by making everything sacred.' Is this a message that Christians communicate well?
- Is there anyone or anything or any activity outside Christ's sacred touch?

# You

Sir John Betjeman's 'Lenten Thoughts of a High Church Anglican' forms a very appropriate reflection for this particular season:

Isn't she lovely, 'the Mistress'?
With her wide-apart grey-green eyes,
The droop of her lips and, when she smiles,
Her glance of amused surprise?

How nonchalantly she wears her clothes,
How expensive they are as well!
And the sound of her voice is as soft and deep
As the Christ Church tenor bell.

But why do I call her 'the Mistress'
Who know not her way of life?
Because she has more of a cared-for air
Than many a legal wife.

How elegantly she swings along
In the vapoury incense veil,
The Angel choir must pause in song

When she kneels at the altar rail.
The preacher said that we should not stare
Around when we come to Church,
Or the Unknown God we are seeking
May forever elude our search.

And I hope that the preacher will not think
It unorthodox and odd
If I add that I catch in 'the Mistress'
A glimpse of the Unknown God.

> Sir John Betjeman, 'Lenten Thoughts of a
> High Church Anglican'

I suppose it is dangerous stuff, daring to see God in 'the Mistress', because it raises a whole gamut of questions about precisely where God is and where God isn't. By and large, we like to set a limit to God and his activity, generally making sure that the line is drawn so that yours truly is safely within his sphere of operations. Certain people act like a prep school master, with God the naughty pupil, pronouncing that some areas are out of divine bounds. Never mind seeing God in the Mistress: for some people the whole of the feminine is a shady area as far as God is concerned, with apoplectic denunciations on subjects ranging from women priests to a woman playing God in a mystery play, from inclusive language to daring to ponder the gender of God him/her/itself.

I came across some of this ire when I published a little book in 1999 called *A Virgin's Diary* – even managing to draw a death threat from Zimbabwe! Having steeped myself in scriptural tradition through 26 years of study, I tried to enter into the mindset of a Mary who was Palestinian, a teenager and pregnant. It wasn't so much the content of the book, but that initial assumption which raised so many hackles.

Yet it is a very veritable tradition, not me, that casts Mary as a young teenager when she gave birth. She was still around at Jesus' death when the average lifespan at that time was two score years, which implies that she gave birth to Jesus at a young age. It has to be remembered that there were no vestal virgins in Israel – there wasn't the tradition that later developed in the West that saw virginity as pure and chaste and lovely. In the harsh world of first-century Palestine, virgins were despised as not having delivered the goods to a threatened nation that needed sons to fight. When Isaiah describes his country as Virgin Israel, he's not flattering her; he's saying she's a useless thing, failing to deliver the very goods she was born for. In a culture where a girl's sole worth was measured in terms of giving birth to children, she did not stay single or a virgin for long.

Yet, despite the truth of all this, many people like

to imagine Mary at the Annunciation as a sort of middle-aged nun and turn a blind eye to a tradition that casts Mary as a teenager and pregnant. Even New Labour demonizes pregnant teenagers. Shockingly, the Gospels deify one.

A few people sneered at my schoolboy approach in writing *A Virgin's Diary*, but, like it or not, it was a school*girl* approach. I tried to imagine the hormonal storm, the establishing of personality and identity, the rebellions that are the *sine qua non* of puberty.

Adolescence is not an optional thing that only happens to bad people. It is an indispensable part of creation, the creation that God either is in or absent from entirely. It is not for us to define and limit his field of play. People who balk at seeing God in Betjeman's Mistress and who don't like their Mary going through all that should question whether or not the incarnation is really for them.

Of course, I also dared to describe a Mary who was not only a teenager, but pregnant, which seemed to me rather a non-negotiable characteristic if God's incarnate son was ever going to stand the chance of seeing the light of day! I imagined all the sickness, fads, cravings, pains, pregnancy and birth that are entirely natural but not, I'm afraid, terribly elegant. Can we tolerate a God made in our elegant image really being there in such a messy thing as pregnancy and birth? Again, he is either there in all his fullness or absent entirely. People who don't like their Mary going through all that (and clearly several people don't), should question if the incarnation is really for them, as Mary herself ponders in this particular extract.

Sunday 7 November

I'm laid up with swollen ankles – leaden, I feel as if I'm carrying the world's woes in my womb. To amuse me Dr Luke smuggled in a statue he'd brought back from his recent forays into the twentieth century. 'Who's this supposed to be, then?' I asked.

'You!' he replied, with a broad grin.

I didn't recognize myself. I looked so serious, so thin, so Italian. Not a bit pregnant. 'Why didn't you bring back "Our Lady of the Swollen Ankles?"' I asked Luke.

'Oh, they're not quite ready for that sort of thing yet,' Luke replied. If they're not quite ready for it after two millennia, I guess they never will be.

David Wilbourne, *A Virgin's Diary*

I wonder if the polarization of opinion about seeing God in things female is part of an age-old debate about panentheism – the determination to see God in every single aspect of his creation, not just in the nice or posh or theologically acceptable bits. Apparently Father Kelly, founder of the Society of the Sacred Mission, which ran a religious order and theological college at Kelham, used to puzzle his visitors by taking them to see the college pigs as a proof of the existence of God. 'If I had shown you stars, flowers, a sunset, you would have said, "How true!" But I do not greatly need God in order to see that beautiful things are beautiful and, well, elevating. I do want to hear of a God who can find a beauty and a joy and an eternal value in my poor pigs' (John Habgood, *Making Sense*).

Even the books of the New Testament are divided on the subject. For instance, Peter's dream in Acts 10.10–16, in pronouncing all foods and creatures clean, seems to be world-affirming (seeing the world as the matrix for God's action). However, 1 John 2.15, which bids us to '. . . not love the world or anything in the world . . .', is undoubtedly world-denying (seeing faith as looking to another country, something other than the world).

The history of Christianity has swung between these two extremes. On the one hand, there is the ultramontane approach, typified by a hemmed-in Rome, denying that there is anything worth encountering beyond the northern mountains and walling itself in to a cosy religious ghetto. On the other hand, there is the approach that engages

35

vibrantly with the secular, anxious to trade with culture, to bring to bear the things of faith in the everyday life of a world that can only be God's. By and large, the ultramontane approach has not led to a time of flourishing, whereas engaging with the secular has. Maybe, though, the ultramontane phases have allowed the Church to regroup and recharge itself for its next engagement with secular culture. It seems we need both approaches to flourish and shouldn't get too fraught about their coexistence, as if one approach denied the other. Maybe each enables the other.

It strikes me that there is a synthesis between the two approaches that I will spell out in the rest of this chapter. Going back to the issue of inclusive language, I can never encounter the current debate about whether God is 'she' without my mother's reproof ringing in my ears. She would pull me up short whenever, as a youngster, I described people carelessly: 'Who's she? The cat's mother?' I suppose she might also have said, 'Who's he? The cat's father?'

The problem for me is not so much ascribing God a gender as describing him in the third person, talking of 'him' as 'he', 'she' or 'it'. When applied to human relationships, talking of people in the third person carries with it a level of distance, often to such a degree that it implies a betrayal:

I left the *Mrs* at 'ome.

*He's* in t' garden.

*She's* burnt my dinner again.

Almost by definition, people in love should encounter one another rather than talk about each other in the third person. It shouldn't be so much, 'I cannot stand *her* cooking!' as 'I cannot stand *your* cooking!' Not so much, '*His* snoring is driving me crazy!' as '*Your* snoring is driving me crazy!'

I do not believe that love is an option, an icing on the cake of existence that can give life a little sparkle. Rather, love is the quintessence of being, the *sine qua non* of humanity itself. Once again, I am tempted to alter Descartes' 'I think, therefore I am' because 'I am loved, therefore I am' seems the order of the Christian day. Becoming does not just happen. For instance, as children, I believe we are loved into being. The squawks are soothed, the parched is wetted, the frozen is warmly tended, the wounds slowly cured as life takes on its fullness and eyes become bright. Probably one of the greatest tragedies in the world is a dull-eyed child who has been deprived of love, that crucial ingredient for life.

Loving children into being applies to teaching as well as parenting. At the last century's start, children were, in the main, seen as empty vessels to be filled with knowledge, with the teacher the stern knowledge-supplier, particularly fierce with wayward vessels who battened down the hatches and refused the cargo. For example, Winston Churchill, in his *My Early Life*, had the audacity to question his Latin master, during a lesson on the vocative case, on how one could possibly address a table, and was severely chastised for his curiosity.

'Then why does Mensa also mean O table,' I enquired, 'and what does O table mean?'

'Mensa, O table, is the vocative case,' he replied.

'But why O table?' I persisted in genuine curiosity.

'O table – you would use that in addressing a table, in invoking a table.' And then seeing he was not carrying me with him, 'You would use it in speaking to a table.'

'But I never do,' I blurted out, in honest amazement.

'If you are impertinent, you will be punished, and punished, let me tell you, very severely,' was his conclusive rejoinder. Such was my first introduction to the Classics from which, I have been told, many of our cleverest men have derived much solace and profit.

Winston Churchill, *My Early Life*

However, we now have a heady alternative with which to travel through the new millennium, where

38

teaching involves being a fellow traveller, both listening and asking. The subject is seen as a far country, to which the teacher has travelled many times so as to be extremely familiar with it. For the pupil it is probably the first trip, so the guide has much to point out. Yet the pupil's role is not just a receptive one – the wonder of the first encounter will make the pupil see things that the rather blasé guide may miss.

Freshness can inform and overcome staleness, making the learning process dynamic and two-way. When the process is one-way, and is fired by a desire to dominate, patronize or control, then it can only fail. Those who see themselves as stern guardians of a moral code to be instilled into their charges whether they like it or not should not be deaf to what those charges themselves can teach them. I think here of how children are more sensitive than adults in caring for the environment.

True teaching involves recognizing the pupil as 'you' rather than treating them as 'it'. To love and be loved means having the courage to recognize the otherness of those around us, those who desperately need both our attention and ministry in order to flourish, those who desire and deserve to be designated 'you' rather than 'he' or 'she' or some other name that denies their personhood. Likewise, we need them to be a 'you' to make us what we are.

All this brings us, as ever, back to God. For encountering the 'you' (lower case) in those around us can only lead us to encounter the ultimate 'You' (upper case), the ground of all our being and our relating. The corollary of 1 John 4.20 – '. . . For anyone who does not love his brother, whom he has seen, cannot love God, whom he has not seen' – is that the one who does love his brother or sister is moving, however hesitantly, towards loving God. 'Whatever you did for one of the least of these brothers of mine, you did for me' (Matthew 25.40). Encountering the other in those around us can only lead to encountering *the* other, who is none other than God.

If it is manifestly wrong to refuse to encounter those around us, demoting them to the third person, it is infinitely more wrong to do so with God, to call him 'she' or 'he' or whatever. Before the new Church of England Prayer Book, *Common Worship*, was passed by the General Synod, there was interminable wrangling about the precise significance in the creed of the Greek word 'εκ, which crops up in the section that explores the doctrine of the incarnation.

'By the power of the Holy Spirit he became incarnate of the Virgin Mary' was ultimately replaced with 'was incarnate from the Holy Spirit and the Virgin Mary'. The new phrase is actually meaningless outside an ecclesiastical culture steeped in patristic theology and lends to the impression that creeds are useless as evangelistic tools. I wonder if the General Synod missed a trick and, while it was into rewriting things, could have opted for a far more radical recasting of the creed's opening words, replacing 'I/we believe in one God' with 'I believe in you', which surely is the ultimate Christian creed, derived from that habit of Jesus' of addressing God as 'abba'.

Although scholars are divided about the origins of the word and its actual usage at the time of Jesus, as we saw earlier, the majority claim 'abba' was the homely Aramaic word for 'daddy'. Significantly, 'daddy' is invariably used in the vocative, the case where 'you' is king, hardly ever in the third person singular:

> 'Daddy, will you cuddle me?'
> 'Daddy, my tummy hurts!'
> 'Daddy, please may I have a drink?'

So it is with Jesus:

> 'Daddy, may your name be held holy.'
> 'Daddy, take this cup away from me.'

Jesus lived and died and rose again not to introduce us to a theological theory, but to champion a relationship with God to which he gave all access. Paul saw such a relationship as typifying life in the Spirit:

> . . . And by him we cry, 'Abba, Father.' The Spirit himself testifies with our spirit that we are God's children. (Romans 8.15–16)

During Lent, I used to take a group of those training for the Church's ministry away for a weekend's retreat at Ampleforth Abbey. The benefits were manifold: inspiring addresses, experiencing being and praying together, tuning in, for a short while, to the daily monastic round of magnificent worship at a Benedictine abbey.

Tragically, one year's retreat was dominated by the suicide of the retreat house warden, whose body was found by one of our number. There was something supremely poignant in that image of an Anglican ordinand, tenderly stooping over the body of a dead Roman Catholic monk. Divided by denomination; united at the point where denomination is irrelevant.

As the group of us sat together – inevitably, devastatingly stunned by it all – my eyes were drawn to the crucifix on the lounge wall. It was an unusual design. Jesus on the cross was definitely in the background. Definitely in the foreground were a man and woman in an embrace almost erotic in its power. Mary the mother of our Lord and John his closest friend were comforting each other:

> Dear woman, here is your son . . . [John], Here is
> your mother. (John 19.26–27)

It is very moving that Jesus took the time, in the
midst of an excruciating death, to attempt to provide comfort for his mother and friend. I wonder,
though, if there is more to it than that. 'Don't stand
there, paralysed by all this, immersed in grief, alone.
Break out of the cocoon and dare to reckon with
each other. Don't gaze at me, dying. Gaze at each
other, and find my life there, risen from the grave.'
The 'You' they encountered (upper case) bade them
to encounter the 'you' (lower case), to find him there.

He speaks the same words to us, both in our grief
and daily round. Truly seeing those around us, and
seeing God there, is the path to resurrection. The
one who encountered God in the quisling, the
woman of the streets, the leper, the dying criminal,
would not have been shocked at Sir John Betjeman
seeing him in the Mistress – or, rather, seeing 'you'.

## Points for reflection:

- What Easter stories are there in the Gospels where
  the resurrection dawns because the disciples
  encounter each other?
- Teaching by sternly filling empty vessels or by
  fellow-travelling. Give an example of these within the Church's life.

- God is either in every aspect of creation or absent entirely. Is there any sphere of activity that you feel is outside God's domain? What would have to change for you to be happy in finding him there?
- 'I believe in you is the ultimate Christian creed.' Should we spend more time talking to God than talking about him?

# 4 We

'We are the body of Christ...' These words are used at modern Communion services to introduce the Peace. Stories about the awkwardness of this practice are manifold. I heard of one venerable lady from a traditional church attending such a service with her daughter. As the Peace was shared, she complained loudly, 'Anne, there's a man at the other side who keeps on touching me!'

I also know of another church where the Peace was shared in a regimented fashion: the celebrant passed the Peace to the churchwardens, who then took a side of the nave each, duly passing it on to the person sitting at the end of each pew. Unfortunately one of the churchwardens was extremely unpopular, which meant that, as the congregation cottoned on to the pattern, her side of the nave tended to be devoid of people.

I heard of another deeply conservative church that annotated its new service books, writing over the section labelled 'The Peace', 'There is no peace here.' This could explain why a visiting celebrant at another deeply conservative church proclaimed,

'The peace of the Lord be always with you. Each of you is now invited to exchange a frosty smile with your neighbour!'

My final example is a church in Liverpool, where the vicar and the congregation had fallen out. At the Peace he stood before them and said, 'I cannot in all honesty share the Peace with you when we are so at variance with each other.' He then sat down in his stall and wept.

We are the body of Christ. How do we express our unity as fellow Anglicans, as fellow Christians albeit in different denominations, as people in relationships within and without the Church? When it comes to unity, Jesus' words from John's Gospel are bandied about in season and out of season, '. . . I pray . . . that all of them may be one, Father, just as you are in me and I am in you. May they also be in us so that the world may believe that you have sent me' (John 17.20–21).

Jesus says these words on the night before he dies. The words of a person in the 24 hours before their death tend to loom large, are given a significance over and above their content. Final words are revered. We tend to fall over backwards to honour the last words of our relatives, words that are often self-evidently ridiculous but to which we are held hostage. People come out with things like, 'Just before he died, Grandad said he wanted a grapefruit placing on his grave and we mustn't let him down.' As they tell us, they nod their heads sagely, as if Grandad had come up with a real gem, the key to life.

Given that we invest so much in what is clearly stupid simply because it is final, it seems shameful that we pay such scant attention to our Lord's final words when they have such wisdom about them. To paraphrase these words, 'That they may be one as we are one': may the unity of God the Father and God the Son be shared by his followers.

The precise nature of that unity is worth pondering. For even a cursory examination of the way the emerging Christian Church spelled out the relationship between the first two persons of the Trinity all too readily indicates that we are not talking about uniformity here. Rather, a substantial degree of difference, paradox or even contradiction was allowed, if not demanded, within the divine relationship between Father and Son.

Just think about the seemingly endless debate about the impassibility of the Father compared to the obvious passibility of the Son, trying to square a transcendent creator God who was omnipotent and not prone to suffering with his Son for whom suffering was a trademark: 'If anyone would come after me, he must deny himself and take up his cross and follow me' (Matthew 16.24). A dawning

perception of the God who was in the crucified
Christ had to be synthesized with the immutable,
inaccessible, passionless God of Greek philosophy.
Unity amid diversity, to coin a phrase, is an under-
statement indeed. A oneness within the Godhead
had to be established within obvious and irreducible
differences, a oneness that Jesus' final words,
according to John's Gospel, bid us to emulate.

As a rather quirky way of looking at such unity,
I would like to explore Jesus' relationship not with
his Father in heaven, but, rather, with his mother
on earth, which seems apt during the period of Lent
when the Christian Church celebrates Mothering
Sunday and the world goes all sentimental and
gooey as it marks its Mother's Day. It strikes me
that there are three key areas of Jesus' relationship
with his mum that offer insight into how to sus-
tain our life together.

The first is the blunt fact that Mary put up with
Jesus when he was off with her.

> . . . She kept the very fountain at her breast;
> The Son adored and nursed by the sweet Maid
> A thousandfold of love for love repaid.
>
> Thomas Ken, 'Her Virgin eyes saw God incarnate born'

It might come as a bit of a shock as you gaze on
innumerable adoring Madonnas cuddling innumerable adoring infants and sing pious hymns about

how well they got on, to be told that this mother and son had their moments. When I mentioned this in a sermon at York Minster, a fundamentalist Christian took me to task afterwards, amazed at my audacity in suggesting that the relationship between Jesus and Mary was anything but perfect. I responded to him on his own ground, drawing his attention to biblical texts, infallible in his view, that certainly did not portray a superson orbiting a supermum.

The first is Jesus' comment to his mother, recorded in John 2.1–11, when she was pestering him to do something about the wine at the wedding feast at Cana. Notoriously difficult to translate, 'τι 'εμοι και σοι, γυναι' goes something like 'What is there between you and me, woman?' Various modern translations have tried to take the sting out of the comment, but without success. Even assuming that John had reproduced Jesus' original words verbatim and hadn't been tempted to sanitize them (as the Gospel writers clearly do elsewhere), we still have a remark that suggests considerable coldness and distance.

That Mary didn't go off in a huff is to her immense credit. Instead, she calmly instructed the stewards, 'Do whatever he tells you', no doubt with eyes rolling to heaven like every long-suffering Jewish momma before and since. Had Mary stomped away when her son was so off with her, we would have been robbed of his first miracle in John's Gospel's scheme of things, and the Prayer Book preface to the marriage service would have lost its punch: 'Which holy estate Christ adorned and beautified with his presence (apart from a major domestic) and first miracle that he would have wrought if only he had listened to his mother, in Cana of Galilee . . .'

Instead, Mary stayed and drove her son to transform what would have been a travesty of a celebration into a joyous surprise. We have to remind ourselves that we are not talking about a mealy-mouthed English wedding here, with sour-looking relatives who could either take the wine or leave it. We are talking about a Palestinian wedding in a land where wine is the staple product, the national emblem, the stuff that really does give joy to the bride and bridegroom, as well as being the only alternative to a rather dodgy water supply. A dry wedding would have been very dry indeed with recriminations abounding.

Mary's insistence, Mary's putting up with what can only be seen as a rebuff, drives Jesus to opt for a generous and joyous surprise rather than the expected misery. This I suppose is her trademark. At the annunciation she boldly opted for God's surprise when any other worldly-wise girl would have plumped for the eminently reasonable alternative: an unequivocal 'no'. She, whose surprising 'yes' to God rescued a world from the sorry state it deserved, drives that surprise throughout her ministry in launching her son. The Mary of surprises is not deterred by the insults from jump-starting the Jesus of surprises.

Another snub is reproduced in the Synoptic Gospels, Mark 3.32 and parallels. In response to the increasing and disturbing criticism by the powers that be that Jesus' mission is being driven by Satan, his family set out to seize him to remove him from harm:

> . . . they told him, 'Your mother and brothers are outside asking for you.' 'Who are my mother and my brothers?' he asked. Then he looked at those seated in a circle around him and said, 'Here are my mother and my brothers! Whoever does God's will is my brother and sister and mother.' (Mark 3.32–35)

OK, Jesus is responding to a threat. OK, the event may have been highlighted, if not overdrawn, by the Early Church, to stress that each disciple is a member of our Lord's family. Even so, Jesus' comment is searingly dismissive of his mother, a mother who gave up so much for him. Remember, she had hardly completed giving birth on a smelly stable floor to a son of dubious paternity before she was condemned to be an asylum seeker by a paranoid Herod. Most mothers would never have let their sons forget that and tolerated no insult, no slight. She did.

> Her Virgin eyes saw God incarnate born,
> when she to Bethlem came that happy morn:
> how high her raptures then began to swell,
> none but her own omniscient Son can tell.
>
> Thomas Ken, 'Her Virgin eyes saw God
> incarnate born'

Certainly her own omniscient son is hiding his rapture very well in this incident, but still she hangs on.

The second area that offers us an insight that we can reflect on to help us in our relationships is that Mary is big enough to let Jesus go. Clearly the incident I have already mentioned, where she and the family set out to snatch Jesus out of harm's way, indicates that this letting go did not occur without a struggle. She wasn't like some laid-back American parent, saying, 'You just be what you've gotta be!' There was a real tension between the God-given desire to protect her offspring and her need to give him space to become.

This tension was there from the outset, with Luke's account of Jesus' birth being overshadowed by Simeon's prophecy, '. . . a sword will pierce your own soul too' (Luke 2.35). This tension is acted out in Luke's description of the 12-year-old Jesus being lost and found again during the Passover festival (Luke 3.41–51). Yet the Jesus Mary finds is no longer a child to be wrapped in her arms, protected, but the Son of God coming of age, sitting with the teachers and asking them questions, astonishing them.

Luke tells us that he went back to Nazareth and was obedient to them, but not smothered by them. It would have been so safe for Mary to have coddled and cosseted him, encouraging him to follow in Joseph's footsteps, a much-respected carpenter-about-town. She had the nerve, albeit eventually, to let him follow in God's footsteps, with his rag-bag of disciples, a path that could only lead to the cross. To return to Alan Paton's 'Meditation for a Young Boy Confirmed', he catches this nerve well in his twelfth stanza:

I see my son is wearing long trousers,
   I tremble at this;
I see he goes forward confidently,
he does not know so fully his own gentleness.
Go forward, eager and reverent child,
see here I begin to take my hands away
   from you,

I shall see you walk careless on the edges of
    the precipice,
but if you wish you shall hear no word come
    out of me;
My whole soul shall be sick with apprehension,
but I shall not disobey you.
Life sees you coming, she sees you coming
    with assurance towards her,
She lies in wait for you, she cannot but
    hurt you;
Go forward, go forward, I hold the bandages
    and ointments ready,
And if you would go elsewhere and lie alone
    with your wounds,
why, I shall not intrude upon you.
If you would seek the help of some other person,
I shall not come forcing myself upon you.

Alan Paton, 'Meditation for a<br>Young Boy Confirmed'

A recipe for our lives together – letting the other
person be, the other Christian be, the other denomination be. Not cloying, not being captive to our
past attempts to control, manipulate, protect, for
the best possible reasons, of course. Rather, giving
ourselves the freedom to let the other, whom we
may have nurtured, be free, topped by our having
the magnanimity to rejoice over the consequences.

'Standing by the cross was his mother.' The third

54

ingredient, the hardest of all, staying through the pain. The bright and promising stars, those who had said they would never betray him, come what may, had all run away on that dark day. She remained, even though it meant heartbreak. To return to Alan Paton's poem, stanza 14 seems appropriate for any parent watching their child – in terms of both letting go and staying with the pain:

Listen to one more word from me,
now that I begin to take my hands from you.
Now God be thanked for this so brief
    possession, so full of joy,
This zest for life, this keen anticipation of
    some quite trivial thing,
This ingenuity for making occupations,
These programs strictly adhered to . . .
. . . These rages, these lunatic stampings,
    these threats of leaving home,
For these withdrawals of affection, when
    you sat pouting like a pigeon,
For these restorations, at all costs to be
    accepted gravely,
even with penitence,
For this reverence, this eagerness, this
    confidence in many persons,
For all these gifts we give our thanks.

Alan Paton, 'Meditation for a<br>Young Boy Confirmed'

Archbishop David Hope was much impressed on a visit to Berlin to encounter a Lutheran pastor who had attended the sabbath eve service at the local synagogue without fail for over 40 years. In the aftermath of World War II and the Holocaust, he had stood with those Jews who remained, not letting his personal and national sense of shame stop him standing with them as they were hurting. That strikes me as the essence of ecumenism.

We are the body of Christ, the Christ who was born of Mary. The relationship between Mary and Jesus has significant parallels with the Benedictine rule, which orders the common life of monastic communities such as Ampleforth here in Yorkshire. Putting up with one another, attending to one another, not taking our bat and ball home and going off in a huff, is the equivalent of the Benedictine rule of obedience. Significantly, in Hebrew and Ancient Greek the forms of the verbs 'to listen' and 'to obey' are very close, if not synonymous. שָׁמַע in Hebrew means both to hear and obey; in Greek ὑποκουειν, to obey, is merely a compound of ἀκουειν, to hear. I sense that we in the West are actually oppressed by too narrow a picture of obedience; we are influenced too much by the image of the automaton under orders being slavishly driven by superiors. We need, instead, to return to the linguistic roots and see obedience in terms of attentiveness, resolving not to shut others out because their behaviour offends us, but be determined to listen to and encourage one another.

Being determined to give the other space to become, and risking the possibility of change rather than preserving the status quo to suit our advantage, equates with the Benedictine rule *conversatio morum* – a phrase that is notoriously difficult to translate but essentially means focusing on an openness to, and ease with, change.

Finally, staying with others even through the pain is mirrored by the Benedictine *stabilitas*. When I first started preaching, I used to trawl through back issues of the *Expository Times*, going back to the safe 1950s, desperately looking for tales to pad my sermons out. One story featured an explorer whose ship was lost in the Atlantic and whose men were parched. Miraculously, they came across another vessel and signalled, 'Give us some of your water, we are dying of thirst!'

Back came the reply, 'Draw the water where you are', which sounded like madness as drinking seawater would only aggravate thirsty men's thirst. They signalled again, more frantically, but were met with the same insane response. When the identical response was made the third time, they decided to chance it, lowered a bucket into the sea and apprehensively tasted it to find it was not salt water, but fresh. They had drifted into the wide mouth of the Amazon.

I didn't go on to speculate how supping from the sewer of South America might have killed them with any of a thousand-and-one diseases, but at least they didn't die of thirst.

In staying by the cross, Mary drew the water where she was – the most bitter of water. Yet this was also the place where God, in the history of the world, has never been more fully present. *Stabilitas* is, of course, the corollary of *conversatio morum*, a paradox rather than a contradiction, a letting go yet simultaneously staying by that Alan Paton catches so masterfully in his poem and Mary catches so mistressfully in her life.

How clever of Mary to anticipate these three cornerstones 500 years before Benedict voiced them. Of course, she wasn't the originator, but caught them from God as he puts up with us, even when we are at our most tedious. God lets us go, doesn't smother us, but allows us to be free, even free to destroy ourselves and him. God, in Christ, stays by us through the pain, doesn't forsake us at Calvary. Instead, he is nailed with us to our cross, carrying us at immense price to the splendour of Easter.

# Points for reflection

- Why do you think sharing the Peace is so awkward in some circles?
- Can you think of three hymns that miss the gospel message by a million miles and three hymns that voice it precisely?
- What other 'difficult' relationships between people in the Bible have been sanitized by church tradition?
- Putting up with each other, letting each other be and staying through the pain – what other ingredients are necessary for good relationships?

# 5 They

I guess a book with chapter titles like mine could not resist quoting Evelyn Waugh's disclaimer in his Author's Note in *Brideshead Revisited*: 'I am not I: thou art not he or she: they are not they.'

Infuriatingly, *they* never are they, in that those who are 'not one of us' just refuse to play our game. Our paranoid imagination may project all sorts of attributes on *them*, may do its best to demonize them, but seldom are we anywhere even remotely near the truth. 'They' are the sitters, we may be the artists, but usually our portrait is at best only a caricature, a silhouette, touching their reality tangentially, if at all. At worst, it is a portrait of the artist himself rather than the sitter, a pastiche of all our prejudices, all the darknesses that we deny are within ourselves but which we are generous to visit on 'them'.

One of the wisest sermons I ever heard was by Rabbi Hugo Gryn who was preaching on the complex book of Jonah. Jonah fiercely resents God's generosity in forgiving the people of Nineveh, the very same rebellious people God sent him to denounce. Yet Jonah's own track record of rebellion is pretty impressive. In being so cross that God is patient and compassionate with the people of Nineveh he seems blind to the fact that God has been infinitely more patient and compassionate with him. It just took Jonah's preaching to turn Nineveh's heart. To turn Jonah, God had to employ a ship and its crew a tempest and a whale (in the course of the Hebrew text it even changes sex, thereby setting the record for the world's first transsexual mammal). A fireworks display of compassion to which Jonah seems oblivious as he spits out his venom about them Ninevites. As Rabbi Gryn concluded, 'We so often try to strangle ourselves by grabbing other people's throats.'

Demarking 'us' and 'them' happens – it is an undoubted fact of life. In many ways, defining ourselves over and against others is an important assertion of our distinct identity. Adolescents define themselves by reacting against their parents, who seem such fuddy-duddies, so stupid that they cannot conceive how they came to conceive them in the first place. Curates define themselves by reacting against their vicars, who seem so out of touch, so arid in their ministry and vocation. New converts define themselves by pouring disdain on cradle Christians, whose faith seems so unexciting and uninspiring, neither hot nor cold. New vicars in the first heady days of an incumbency can develop a messiah complex, defining themselves by rubbishing their predecessors – they were so tired, so lacklustre, so lacking in the Spirit: 'They who were before me were thieves and robbers; I am the one who is to come!'

It happens. We all play at making ourselves look big by making 'them' look so small, especially when we are under threat, unsure, insecure. Even Jesus plays the game, with his:

> Woe to you, teachers of the law and Pharisees, you hypocrites! You are like whitewashed tombs, which look beautiful on the outside but on the inside are full of dead men's bones and everything unclean. In the same way, on the outside you appear to people as righteous but on the inside you are full of hypocrisy and wickedness. (Matthew 23.27–28)

I love him all for more for his saying that. So angry. So human. Thank God that the Church of England Communications Office didn't nobble and sanitize him with: 'While there is a great deal about the Pharisees that I admire and, indeed, wished I personally could live up to, I do wonder about one or two points where their actions seem, to me, to be slightly at variance with their manifesto. I fully allow, though, that I may have misunderstood them and wish them every blessing as they seek God's will in the way that seems best to them.'

Yet he didn't stick in a venomous rut, but worked through all that. As the Gospels take us through Holy Week 'Woe to them' becomes 'Father, forgive them . . .' as they did their very worst to him. Surely Jesus presents a calling to us, for us to work through all that, too, travel with him on his *via dolorosa* on a journey of the heart, so that we can move on from belittling them to forgiving them.

I can't help thinking of Jesus' response when 'they' were getting at him on another occasion: 'Is it lawful to pay taxes to Caesar, or not?' He draws their attention to the superscription on the tribute money, then gives his measured response, which has resonated through the centuries – 'Give to Caesar what is Caesar's, and to God what is God's' (Matthew 22.21).

The Jerusalem Bible paraphrases that verse as 'Give back to God what belongs to God', which was a bit of a revolutionary's charter because, according to the salvation history unfolded in the Hebrew scriptures, Israel herself belonged to God, the Holy Land he promised from Abraham to the Exodus to give to his people, the Jews. That Promised Land and its resources were emphatically not Caesar's, but God's, and therefore were simply not at any Caesar's disposal, be that Caesar Roman or any other Gentile.

The two centuries before Christ provided a rich tapestry of Jewish heroes who had stood up against Greek and then Roman oppression, the Maccabean martyrs inspiring the zealots of Jesus' day. Less than 40 years after Jesus' death, the city of Jerusalem refused to hand over her tribute money to Rome, her taxes to Caesar. That refusal was one of the reasons for war, the cruellest of wars that resulted in the Jewish nation being dismantled.

Every war has its dark images that outlast it, such as the Somme, Mons, Coventry, Dresden, Hiroshima in the last century. The first century's dark icon is the high fortress of Masada, ominously overlooking the Dead Sea. There, Jewish nationalists holed themselves in, hopelessly outnumbered by the Roman army that besieged them. Every man, woman and child committed suicide en masse rather than sue for peace with their pagan enemies, believing they were better dead than betray or compromise the promise that the land was theirs. 'Back to God what belongs to God' was a fiercely held revolutionary's charter indeed.

That revolutionary's charter can be extrapolated far beyond Palestine and the Roman Empire. In a world that is increasingly seen as promised and

God-given, our rage seems rightly directed at 'them', they who have the audacity to usurp God's authority. How dare 'they' pollute the seas! How dare 'they' hoard their wealth! How dare 'they' trigger global warming! How dare 'they' inflict misery on millions! How dare 'they' threaten nuclear holocaust!

All heady stuff, but with one fatal flaw. If we say, quite rightly, that God's sphere is limitless, then Caesar belongs to God, too. There's a certain irony in it all. We rightly liberate God from the narrow confines of 'religion' or 'church', we rightly proclaim that Jesus' ministry and mission was to abolish the sacred by making everything sacred, yet we can't both liberate God and restrict him at the same time. If we believe Jesus conferred a sacredness on every-thing, if we believe God's Spirit breathes through the whole world, we can't then confine that Spirit to ourselves and the people and issues who share our prejudices. If we celebrate God's Spirit breathing within us, we have to allow that same Spirit to breathe within 'them', even Caesar. To write off a Caesar, to write off any leader, to write off 'them' as ungodly or unchristian is thereby to cut ourselves off from the source of our being. If we choose to limit God's generosity, who's to say on which side of our self-drawn line we are actually on?

Second Isaiah got it profoundly right when he cut

across the narrow nationalism that was to loom in Israel's later history and dared to call Cyrus God's anointed (Isaiah 45.1). Obviously he had a vested interest in doing that as the spin-off from Cyrus' conquest of Babylon was that the Jews enslaved there were liberated. However, this was only a spin-off. Cyrus was no benign and liberal saviour – he was capable of tremendous cruelty. He was the original storm from the East, who got Persia's act together and put paid to mighty enemies across all her borders. For instance, in his campaign against the ancient kingdom of Lydia, his troops were ordered to kill, without mercy, every single Lydian they met – man, woman and child. In his *Histories*, Herodotus, who was by no means unsympathetic to Cyrus, describes how the conqueror set out to burn alive Lydia's King Croesus, who was tied to a pyre with 14 young Lydian boys. For some reason, Cyrus then changed his mind, but the fire had taken too firm a hold. Fortunately, a convenient downpour, which Herodotus interpreted as the interceding tears of Apollo, saved the day and Croesus was released from the damp embers, from then onwards employed by Cyrus as a quisling, giving advice on how to subjugate his people.

'This is what the Lord says to his anointed, to Cyrus, whose right hand I take hold of . . .' (Isaiah 45.1). To describe this tyrant as the Lord's anointed was a bold statement for Isaiah to make, to say the least. It becomes even bolder when you dig behind the rather tame English and uncover the original Hebrew scriptures and Greek Septuagint where we find, 'Thus says the Lord to Cyrus, his mashiach, his messiah', 'Thus says the Lord to his χριστος, his Christ.' OK, the messianic roadshow hadn't gathered that much momentum five centuries before Jesus, but, even so, to call a Persian barbarian a messiah, a Christ was an undoubted accolade, especially when you recall that Jewish prophets didn't get all that excited about their own kings, let alone foreign ones. When set against Israel's subsequent sharply xenophobic history, with a choosiness bordering on the finicky about the messiah's precise Jewish credentials, the courage of Second Isaiah's accolade seems all the more remarkable. How would we react to texts such as:

This is what the Lord says to his anointed, to Hitler, whose right hand I take hold of . . .

This is what the Lord says to his anointed, to Saddam Hussein, whose right hand I take hold of . . .

This is what the Lord says to his anointed, to Milosevic, whose right hand I take hold of . . .

Shocking stuff indeed. Sheer boldness such as

67

Second Isaiah's can only signify a span of God's activity that is infinite, without limit: '. . . I am the Lord, and there is no other. I form the light and create darkness, I bring prosperity and create disaster; I, the Lord, do all these things' (Isaiah 45.6–7). If he was there in Cyrus, he was there in Caesar and is there in 'them', our present-day rulers. Whether they like it or not and whether we like it or not, there he is.

If we don't like it, if we blatantly refuse to allow him to be with 'them' when they are such blatantly tedious and obnoxious people, then why on earth should he have bothered with such blatantly tedious and obnoxious us in the first place? In walling off ourselves in a secure ghetto far away from 'them', it is not only ourselves whom we disenfranchise. We should be mindful of the one who remains outside the city wall, breathing his last, saying, 'Father, forgive them, for they know not what they do.'

Being mindful of him should shape our actions. I recall a Bible study about forgiveness that I led in Middlesbrough just after I had been ordained. My perhaps rather naive plea for a conciliatory approach to those we deemed our enemies was interrupted by an angry old man who said, 'Let me tell you, lad, I fought in the last war in the Far East and was captured and tortured by the Japanese. They were utter fiends. I'll never forget or forgive. Forty years on, if

I saw a group of Japanese tourists walking down this street, I'd kill the lot of them, I tell you, I hate them so much.'

I repeated the words our Lord addressed to his torturers from the cross, torturers equally as fiendish. 'That's no help to me,' he responded, still driven by fierce anger. 'He was a superman. I'm only human. I can't forgive, I tell you.' The rest of the study group nodded and clucked sympathetically. I feared their vote lay with the angry man's view rather than mine.

Yet I feel that if the sort of forgiveness Christ championed on the cross is of no earthly use to us, then we of all people are most to be pitied. Rather than coming across at his crucifixion as a superman, Jesus seems so essentially human – hurting, betrayed, battling with darkness, feeling an abandonment so massive that even God seems to have forsaken him. That he is able to gasp from that forlorn base, 'Father, forgive them', strikes me as offering a way forward for us all.

Another person who was severely tortured by the Japanese was Leonard Wilson, Bishop of Singapore. In his book *Martyrs of Our Time*, William Purcell reproduces the transcript of a radio talk Bishop Wilson gave following World War II in which he addresses mightily the subject of how we can glimpse in our own lives Christ's ability to forgive:

In the middle of the torture, they asked me if I still believed in God. When by God's help I said 'I do', they asked me why God did not save me, I said, 'God does save me. He does not save me by freeing me from pain or punishment; but he saves me by giving me the spirit to bear it.' When they asked me why I did not curse them, I told them it was because I was a follower of Jesus Christ, who taught us that we were all brethren. I did not like to use the words, 'Father, forgive them.' It seemed too blasphemous to use our Lord's words. But I felt them and I said, 'Father, I know these men are doing their duty. Help them to see I am innocent.' And when I muttered, 'Father, forgive them', I wondered how far I was being dramatic and if I really meant it, because I looked at their faces as they stood around and took it in turns to flog, and their faces were hard and cruel and some of them were evidently enjoying their cruelty.

But by the grace of God, I saw those men not as they were, but as they had been. Once they were little children playing with their brothers and sisters and happy in their parents' love, in those far off days before they had been conditioned by their false nationalist ideals, and it is hard to hate little children.

But even that was not enough. There came

into my mind as I lay there that Communion hymn,

> Look Father, look on his anointed face,
> And only look on us as found in him;
> Look not on our misusings of thy grace,
> Our prayer so languid, our faith so dim;
> For lo, between our sins and their reward
> We set the Passion of thy Son our Lord.

And so I saw them, not as they were, not as they had been, but as they were capable of becoming, redeemed by the power of Christ, and I knew it was only common sense to say, 'Forgive.'

Bishop Leonard Wilson, *Martyrs of Our Time*

Seeing 'them' as little children; seeing 'them' as they might become in Christ seems to be one recipe for transforming 'them' into 'us'. In our own heads and in their heads as well. Legend has it that returning to ministry in Singapore after the war, Bishop Wilson looked into the eyes of a Japanese candidate he was confirming and was startled to see his former torturer. Wilson's determination, despite torture, to see even his enemies as brothers and sisters in Christ had not just worked for his salvation, but for his enemy's as well, who had been moved to leave behind his former 'false nationalist ideal' and embrace the whole of humanity as the body of Christ.

Two thousand years before, the narrowly zealous Paul had witnessed Stephen praying for forgiveness for those who stoned him, an incident that he must have pondered on long, until the penny dropped and the blinding light dawned on the Damascus road. Then he, too, not only embraced the whole of humanity as the body of Christ, but also actually formulated the entire doctrine! Allowing 'them' to become 'us' can have some remarkable consequences.

The process is a two-way one, being generous to those who are other than us in including them rather than excluding them, hoping that our generosity might spur them on to be generous, too. As we humbly mutter, 'Father, forgive them', we might add, 'Father, forgive us for making them "them" and not having the nerve to welcome them as "us".'

That, though, would produce a sentence more complex than Evelyn Waugh's disclaimer with which we began. When it comes to the subject of forgiveness, we don't need complex sentences; we just need to get on with it. I recall an open-air service during a chilly Scarborough summer in 1971, addressed by a curious duet consisting of Dana, the Irish pop singer, and Donald Coggan, then Archbishop of York. After Dana had trilled 'All kinds of everything remind me of you' (maybe with a subtext about transforming 'them' into 'us'), the

Archbishop made an impassioned plea for forgiveness: 'When you go home tonight, make a phone call, write a letter, say a word and forgive someone. I plead with you: forgive them with all your heart.'

## Points for reflection

- 'Give back to God what belongs to God.' What area of our life deserves recovery for God?
- Transforming 'them' into 'us' by the act of forgiveness. Who can we do that with:
  – in our national life
  – in our world
  – in our personal relationships?
- Taking a trawl through history, what other world despots could be described as God's Christ?
- Think of examples of the ghetto mentality in our community and our Church.
- Who beckons to us to leap over the walls that constrain us?

# 6     Me

A businessman was in trouble. Several creditors had failed to pay up and he was teetering on the brink of bankruptcy. In desperation, he went into a nearby church and prayed, 'Why me, Lord? Help me out of this mess. Let me win the Lottery.' Silence.

The man's troubles worsened. His business was liquidated, his workers made redundant, his expensive home was threatened with repossession. He returned to the church and uttered the same prayer, but it was still met with silence.

Things deteriorated further. His wife left him. He lost his home, his expensive possessions. However, clinging to one tiny chance that he still might recover everything, he went to the church one last time. 'Why me, Lord? Help me out of this mess. Let me win the Lottery.'

This time the Lord spoke back, saying 'OK, OK, I'll help, I'll help. You can win the Lottery, but how about meeting me halfway? For goodness sake, this time, buy a ticket!'

'Why me?' is a question that has never loomed so

large. In a society where I like to be in control, I like to be the initiator, I like to be independent, it is hard to be kept waiting on tenterhooks, forced to depend, assailed by illness, tragedy or grief totally beyond my control, to be treated as a 'me' rather than an 'I'.

We may have put up with all those endless queues for rations in World War II, but we don't like it now, whether it be queuing on a National Health waiting list or queuing in a traffic jam. Surely being a victim belongs to the vicissitudes of a previous age or more primitive cultures, when humanity was more at the mercy of climate, war, crop failure, natural disaster, rampant disease, sheer ignorance. We've come of age now; we have moved into a new phase where having things happen to me should have been eradicated, along with smallpox. It seems most undignified to be cast as a victim; not what being human is about at all. For these reasons we shy away from passivity.

I really do wonder about our prevailing obsession with activity. 'What do you watch on TV?' I generally ask people when I visit them. The entire layout of their living room will be focused on the television set. 'Oh, we hardly ever watch TV, Vicar, hardly ever. Well, just those marvellous nature programmes David Attenborough does.' Very expensive programmes, as, just for them, it appears, they fork out a small fortune for all the latest high-tech equipment and ever-increasing licence fee.

Why do they feel they have to apologize to me for adopting the passive role of watching? Is it some hangover from the Protestant work ethic synthesized with a hyperactive Thatcherism, a fear of being thought idle, not active enough to earn salvation?

Don't get me wrong, because I'm judging myself here as much as those I visit. I know that if I'm sitting at home, reading a book, if the doorbell rings I immediately leap about my study, shuffling the papers on my desk, trying to look as if I was doing something. 'I'm sorry to interrupt you when you must be so busy, Vicar,' the caller apologizes. I try to give a weary smile, my own false sacrifice to the idol of busyness.

There's a joke going around where a curate bustles up to his vicar who is idling in the sanctuary. 'Father, there's a tramp just come in at the back of church who says he's almighty God,' he informs his boss. The vicar gives the vagrant a long stare. 'I don't think he is,' he concludes. 'But, just in case, we'd better look busy!'

Why do we have to look busy? Why do we take our cue from Martha, whose hyperactivity and bustling about infuriated Jesus, rather than from

Mary, who had the nerve simply to sit and wait and listen, and in so doing received our Lord's accolade?

Cosmo Gordon Lang made the following telling observation in 1929 as he reflected on his two decades as Archbishop of York:

> I look back to the beginning of my time as Archbishop and think of all the hopes and plans with which I began. And now, after 20 years, the ending. Certainly there was enough and to spare of doing. Yet, after all the ceaseless process of doing, what was actually done? Church life somewhat encouraged and invigorated, I hope . . . but how many souls were brought nearer to God by all this doing? The words of the Methodist hymn come to mind, 'Doing is a deadly thing.' What is certain is that much more of true value might have been done if I had cared less for doing and more for being. If the inner life had been kept more true, the outer life would have borne more fruit. 'He that abideth in Me and I in him,' said the Lord, 'the same bringeth forth much fruit. For apart from Me you can do nothing.'
>
> J. G. Lockhart, *Cosmo Gordon Lang*

The trial, suffering and death of Jesus confers a status on 'doing nothing' that should offset our fretting about always having to be active. It is very significant that he allows himself to be handed over, to be treated as a victim, to be *led* like a sacrificial lamb to the slaughter.

We have a tendency to see such tragic events as things that shouldn't have happened, that should never have been part of the script – 'Why me?' is voiced abroad once again. Alternatively, we take a laid-back view – 'It happens,' we say, with a transatlantic drawl to our voice as we shrug our shoulders, implying that nothing has any purpose, any point.

I contend that Jesus' suffering and death didn't just happen; it was written into the plot from the very beginning, written into the world from the very beginning. That's one of the flaws of the rock musical *Godspell* in that it casts Jesus as a sort of Aesop par excellence, very much into frenzied activity, cavorting around Palestine, telling amazing stories that hold his adoring followers spellbound. Then, inexplicably, he is put to a messy death in a puzzling final scene.

His being handed over to death was not inexplicable. Anyone who proclaimed God's total and unreserved accessibility within a religious system that thrived on meting out God's approval and disapproval could only seal their doom. Anyone who encouraged his disciples to eat meals with defiled hands in a culture where concern about food preparation was as high on the agenda as marching is to an Orangeman was asking to be lynched. Anyone who urged, 'You must love your enemies' on a people spoiling for revolt and an occupying power whose brute force was its trademark risked the outrage of both. Anyone who prophesied 'Destroy this temple and I will raise it up again in three days' was simply courting trouble – the temple was such an icon of nationalistic pride that even a whiff of criticism was taboo. Anyone who preached, 'The Kingdom of God is upon you!' to those who had a vested interest in keeping God well out of it, thank you very much, should not have been surprised when they tried to shut him up for good. He must have seen it coming. Yet, with joy, Jesus set his face towards Jerusalem: 'Now is the time for the Son of man to be handed over...'

He acts all that out on Palm Sunday, as recorded in John's Gospel (John 12.12–14). Significantly, in the other three Gospels, Jesus climbs on an ass and then the crowd greets him as king – the scene echoing the prophet Zechariah, 'Behold your king is coming to you, humble and mounted on an ass.' However, in John's Gospel, it's the other way round. The crowd sets out to greet him, to hail him as its king, to pin a label on him, to fit him into a slot, to constrain him within the old, known ways. Jesus will have none of it. It is at this point, in response to them, that he takes a donkey and sits on it. 'I'

79

proclaims itself 'me'. Control gives way to no control, as a beast of burden takes the initiative. The Word made flesh, from whom all words, all creation itself, originate, is enthroned: a victim.

He chooses to be vulnerable; he does not have it thrust on him by accident. Traditional teaching about God asserts that it is his nature to be impassible – that is, it is not dictated that he should suffer. God could hardly be God if he was, by definition, at the mercy of that which he created and creates. However, equally by definition, God cannot be constrained by the limitations of our theology, nor is he inherently at the mercy of our philosophical systems. We can theorize for ever about what God is like and what he is not like, but, in the end, we have to let him be, let him be the God who might be a million miles from our pat theories. 'He is such a fast God, always before us and leaving as we arrive' is R. S. Thomas' description in his poem, 'Pilgrimages'. Ours is not a God who can be sealed in a tomb or locked up in our neat theological theories. He can choose to suffer, he can choose to put himself at our mercy. Who are we to say otherwise? The unthinkable can actually be thought; the unlovable can actually be loved (even the most oily politicians have wives!); the impassible can actually resign itself to passivity.

Why? It's a funny thing to do, surely, risking it all

when you've got the whole of existence going for you. Why the death wish, God? Why should 'the maker of the stars and sea become a child on earth for me?' If you prefer Graham Kendrick to John Betjeman, why should 'the one who threw stars into space to cruel nails surrender'? If Kendrick and Betjeman present a too modern cocktail and your preference is for old-timers like Thomas Aquinas, why is God 'given for us and condescending to be born for us below'?

For love. He did it all for love. You can do a lot as 'I', initiating, striding around being the subject, so busy, so busy. I can have prophetic powers. I can have all faith. I can give away all I have. I can even be burned for my beliefs. If I have not love, however, I am nothing. To love means letting 'I' become 'me'. Strutting about like a colossus or champing at the bit for some important activity to turn up, gives way to waiting for love, waiting for the lover to either respond to me or reject me.

Unless you only want to be loved by an automaton, you cannot prescribe love, money can't buy you that love, you cannot order the other to respond and return your love. If you do, then what is returned is not love but merely obeisance. To love and be loved, you have to wait. In a curious way, the date who has been stood up and spends minute after minute futilely waiting outside the cinema or some other assignation, actually defines the quality of love he or she has been denied. Someone can have a faith that moves mountains and give all he possesses to the poor, but if he does not wait for his beloved to respond, he has not love.

This reminds me how Abraham's oldest and most trusted servant in Genesis 24 simply had to wait on Rebekah's response at the well, on which so much was at stake. Not just the good opinion of his master in his old age. Not just the allaying of Abraham's deep anxiety about finding his son a proper wife, but the whole future of Jewish nationhood, which God had promised through Abraham's descendants, hinged on that moment. Was it to be Rebekah, wife of Isaac? Was it to be Rebekah, mother of Jacob, who became Israel? Was it to be Rebekah, grandmother of Jacob's 12 sons who became Israel's patriarchs or not? The servant could only wait.

Was it that same servant who, years earlier, had had to be content just to wait while Abraham and his infant son had trudged up the fateful mountain in Moriah, bearing the kindling for sacrifice, hoping against hope that the father would do his son no harm? All he could do was wait, pray that Abraham would come to his senses and hear the God of tenderness rather than the murderous god of his imagination.

82

We all have to wait, too. You have to put yourself at their mercy. 'I' has to be 'me'. 'Why me?' is
not some blip on the canvas of existence, it is the
essence of it. *Sine qua non*, without which not. Even
Jesus had to wait on the responses of those around
him. The real agony in the Garden of Gethsemane
was as Jesus waited to see if those who came with
their lanterns and clubs were friends or foes.

> Jesus . . . asked them, 'Who is it you want?'
> 'Jesus of Nazareth,' they replied.
> 'I am he', Jesus said . . . When Jesus said 'I am
> he', they drew back and fell to the ground. (John
> 18.4–6)

So runs John's account of the arrest of Jesus in the
Garden of Gethsemane, the moment when Jesus,
the waiting Son of God, voluntarily hands himself
over. At that very moment, those who came to arrest
him fell to the ground. Undoubtedly, Jesus' words,
'I am he' echoed Yahweh, the Hebrew Tetragram-
maton for God, so terrible, so sacred, that it was
blasphemy even to utter it. The arresting party fell
on their faces in fear. It sounds a trifle *Life of
Brian*ish, with every petty criminal in first-century
Palestine invoking the divine name and making
good his escape while his arresters lay prostrate.

However, I sense that there is something more,
raising this episode above the Monty Pythonesque.

83

That, in some primitive way, those who came to arrest Jesus recognized, in the moment of his handing himself over, the essence of the divine. They could only fall down on their faces, in total and utter awe. This was love, naked, vulnerable, the heart of God.

As Jesus' story draws to its end, there are striking parallels here with one story of his beginning, where the wise men from the East, in Matthew's Gospel, prostrate themselves and worship the baby waiting for them in Mary's arms (Matthew 2.11). In that helpless child they saw God, whose very name is love, in all his fullness.

Of course, those arresting Jesus got up again and did their very worst to him as he was bound and led away. The dark night features a mosaic of utter cruelty: the humiliating trial before the high priest and all his sidekicks, railing against their solitary vulnerable prisoner; the accusations, evidently false but made searing none the less by the venom with which they were spat out; the blows, delivered by fighting men whose trade was to inflict pain, severe, dehumanizing pain. Watching it all was Peter, his best friend, his trump card, the one who said he would himself risk death to come to Jesus' rescue, in the event denying he'd ever come across him, warming his hands by the cosy fire while his Lord shivered with fear.

This heartbreaking cruelty was epitomized by the crown of thorns rammed on to his head, tearing his scalp. At Bishopthorpe Palace, one of the trophies a former archbishop of York had brought back from his travels was a crown of thorns made from an African thorn tree. It was on display in the chapel and, when conducting a guided tour, I always ended by drawing visitors' attention to it. Hitherto, the tour had been a gentle one, with the visitors cooing at all the nice historical features of the palace, so English, so cosy, with any awkward, nasty details mentioned briefly in passing, safely separated from us by centuries. I gingerly picked up the crown – the thing was capable of severely wounding your hand with just the merest touch – lifted it up in the air and rammed it down. 'Ladies and gentlemen,' I would conclude. 'This is the real reason for this place being here. Something very like this would be thrust on his uncovered, unprotected head. He went through all that and worse for you and for me, simply to show he loved us.' Everyone then left to wander around the grounds, looking considerably paler than when they had come in.

Finally came the nails tearing his flesh, the hanging there, outside the city wall on the city rubbish dump, dark and alone. There was no escaping the possibility of such rejection, awful in its totality. God could hardly wave a magic wand and send his legions of angels, saying, 'Stop, stop, I was only playing at love. Actually I'm in control, so put away your whips and your crowns of thorns and your crosses and leave him alone. Leave "me" alone.'

He could not do that and still be love. He had to be 'me'. The Passion gives us a window into God, the God of love, who has been 'me' since the very foundation of the world. The trumpets of Easter, faintly sounding on Good Friday, remind us that, even when love is so totally rejected, God will not give up. His persistence will breathe triumph into the direst tragedy.

Those men who fell down and got up again: I wonder if afterwards they were at ease in the old dispensation, where 'I' was king, or would they give way to being 'me' and be met by God in the wounding and the waiting? This seems to be a cue for R. S. Thomas, to both end and begin.

> Moments of great calm,
> Kneeling before an altar
> Of wood in a stone church
> In summer, waiting for the God
> To speak; the air a staircase
> For silence; the sun's light
> Ringing me, as though I acted
> A great role. And the audiences
> Still; all that close throng

Of spirits waiting, as I
For the message.
Prompt me, God;
But not yet. When I speak,
Though it be you who speak
Through me, something is lost.
The meaning is in the waiting.

R. S. Thomas, 'Kneeling'

## Points for reflection

- Can you think of any examples in the Old Testament of God being cast as a victim?
- Can you think of any examples in Scripture or in the history of the Christian Church where waiting has been a key feature?
- In what sense can you see prayer as a waiting for God or God waiting for us?
- Why do we in the West get so impatient about being kept waiting?

# Bibliography

Betjeman, Sir John, *Collected Poems*, John Murray, 1958

Churchill, Winston, *My Early Life*, Oldham's Press, 1949

Farrer, Austin, *A Celebration of Faith*, Hodder & Stoughton, 1970

Habgood, John, *Making Sense*, SPCK, 1993

Hughes, Gerard, *God of Surprises*, Darton, Longman & Todd, 1985

Lockhart, J. G., *Cosmo Gordon Lang*, Hodder & Stoughton, 1949

Paton, Alan, *Meditation for a Young Boy Confirmed*, *Theology*, August 1958

Potter, Dennis, *Son of Man*, Penguin, 1971

Purcell, William, *Martyrs of Our Time*, Mowbray, 1983

Thomas, R. S., *Collected Poems 1945–1990*, Phoenix Giant, 1995

Thomas, R. S., *Later Poems 1972–1982*, Macmillan, 1983

Wilbourne, David, *A Virgin's Diary*, Azure, 1999